FOUR SQUARE

KARA L. LAUGHLIN

Published by The Child's World®
1980 Lookout Drive • Mankato, MN 56003-1705
800-599-READ • www.childsworld.com

Photo Credits
© Eric Isaacs/emiphoto.com: 5, 8-9, 10, 14,
16-17, 18-19; Joel Blit/Shutterstock.com: 6-7;
Jupiterimages/Getty: cover, 21; ZUMA Press, Inc./
Alamy Stock Photo: 12-13

ISBN: 9781503823723
LCCN: 2017944893

Printed in the United States of America
PA2356

ABOUT THE AUTHOR

Kara L. Laughlin is an artist and
writer who lives in Virginia with her
husband, three kids, two guinea
pigs, and a dog. She is the author of
two dozen nonfiction books for kids.

TABLE OF CONTENTS

Time to Play! . . . 4

A Place to Play . . . 7

Ready, Set... . . . 8

Serve! . . . 11

Bouncing Action . . . 13

In and Out. . . 15

You're Out! . . . 16

Moving Up . . . 19

Victory! . . . 20

Glossary . . . 22

To Learn More . . . 23

Index . . . 24

TIME TO PLAY!

Get some friends and a kickball. It's time to play four square!

FUN FACT

The longest game of four square was played in Buenos Aires, Argentina. It lasted 29 hours.

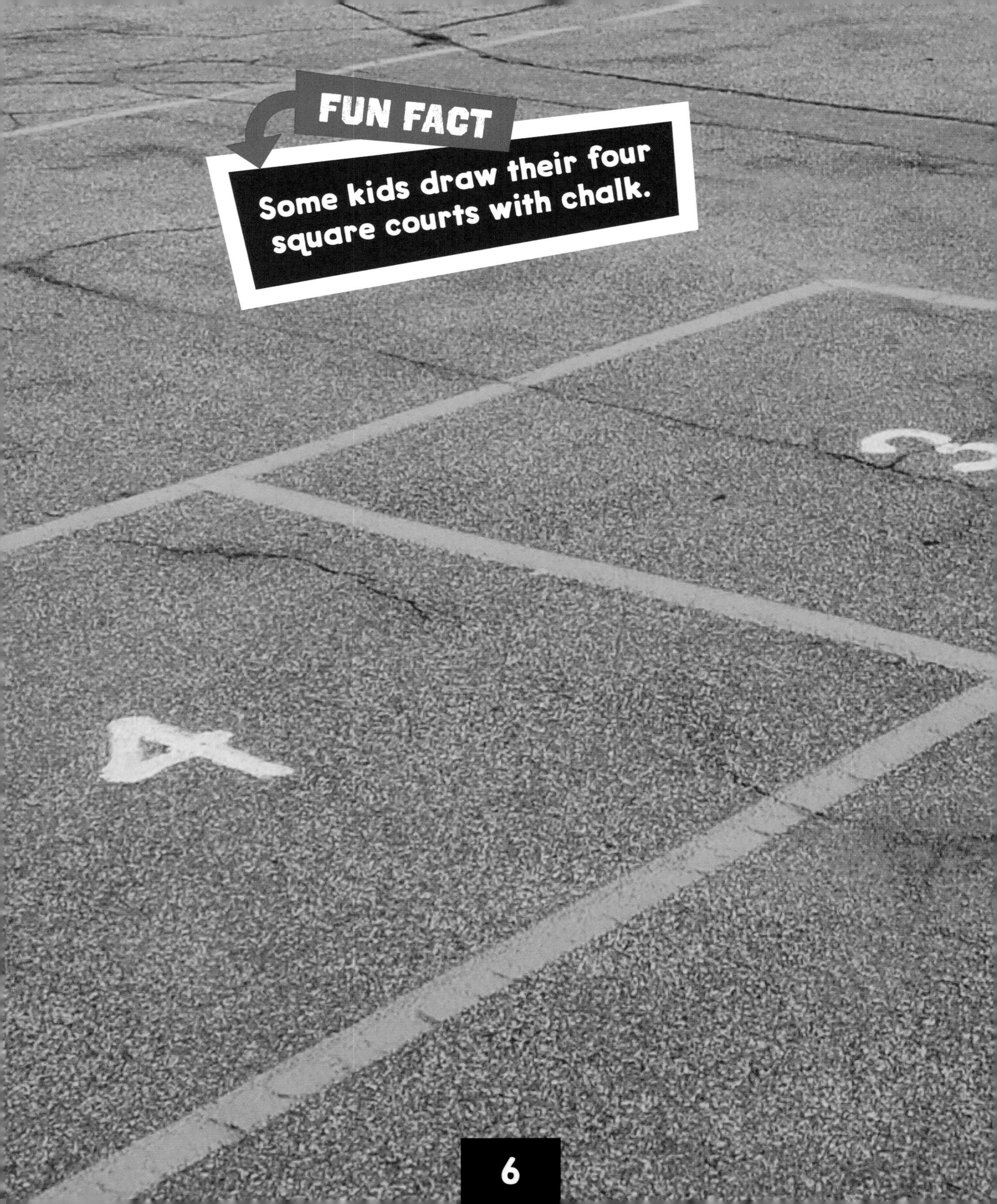

FUN FACT

Some kids draw their four square courts with chalk.

A four square **court** is one big
square split into four boxes.
Many schools and parks have
four square courts.

One player stands in each box. The boxes are **ranked** 1, 2, 3, and 4. The person in the highest box gets to **serve**.

The server stands in the far corner of box 4. He bounces the ball in his box. He hits it diagonally across the court.

FUN FACT

Some courts have a square or triangle in box 4. It shows where to stand for the serve.

BOUNCING ACTION

The ball bounces into a player's box. He can hit it to any other box.

Q: If I'm out, I'm in.
If I'm in, I'm out. What am I?
A: A four square court line.

IN AND OUT

The court has two kinds of lines: **Outside lines** make the big square. The lines that make the boxes are **inside lines**.

If a ball hits an outside line, it is **in**. If a ball hits an inside line, it is **out**.

Players hit the ball back and forth until a player is out. She might miss the ball. She might hit it out. Or the ball could bounce twice.

Some four square rules change from place to place. Players agree on the rules before each game.

In bigger games, other players wait in line. When a player is out, he goes to the end of the line. The first person in line enters the game at box 1.

When a player is out, she goes back to box 1. The players below her move up one rank. The server scores one point.

VICTORY!

At the end of the game, the person with the most points wins!

FUN FACT

In 2009, 3,176 players set the record for most people playing four square at once. Forty-four US schools took part.

GLOSSARY

court (KORT): The square area where the game is played.

in (IN): Still inside the court. A ball that is "in" is still in play.

inside line (IN-syd LINE): The cross-shaped lines that break up the court into four boxes.

out (OWT): Not inside the court. A ball that is "out" ends play.

outside line (OWT-syd LINE): The large square line that marks the outside boundary of the court.

rank (RANK): The order in which players progress. Players come into the game at box 1 and move up to box 4.

server (SUR-vur): The player who hits the ball to put it into play. The only player who can score points.

TO LEARN MORE

In the Library

Bozzo, Linda. *At Play in the Past, Present and Future*. New York, NY: Enslow Publishing, 2011.

KaBOOM! *Go Out and Play*. Somerville, MA: Candlewick Press, 2012.

On the Web

Visit our Web page for lots of links about four square:

childsworld.com/links

Note to parents, teachers, and librarians: We routinely verify our Web links to make sure they are safe, active sites—so encourage your readers to check them out!

INDEX

ball, 11, 15, 16
bouncing, 13, 16
boxes, 7, 8, 11, 13, 15, 19
Buenos Aires, 4

chalk, 6
court, 6, 7, 12, 14, 15

in, 15
inside lines, 15

lines, 14, 15
longest game, 4

out, 15, 16, 19
outside lines, 15

players, 8, 16
points, 19, 20

serve, 8, 11
server, 8, 9, 19

winning, 20